Down the Mississippi

By Howard Gutner

CONTENTS

CELEBRATION PRESS

Pearson Learning Group

America's Big River

One of the biggest and longest rivers in the United States starts as a tiny stream of water in northern Minnesota. It is so small at this point that you could almost jump across it! As it moves south, though, it collects water from other rivers that flow into it. Through ten states the stream swells and grows into a mighty river. Finally it empties into the Gulf of Mexico, 2,340 miles from where it began.

The mighty Mississippi River flows through St. Louis, Missouri.

The Mississippi River begins in Lake Itasca in northern Minnesota, and then flows south to the Gulf of Mexico.

Native Americans named this river *Meschasipi,* or "Big Water." English-speaking settlers turned the name into "Mississippi." Others have called it Old Muddy, Old Man River, or the Mighty Mississippi.

It is one of the world's busiest rivers. Ships carry products such as cotton, coal, and oil to its port cities. From the Gulf of Mexico, these ships can sail on to the Atlantic Ocean.

A young
Abraham Lincoln
poles a flatboat
on the Mississippi.

The great river is more than just a water highway, though. It has also played a big part in American history. As a young man Abraham Lincoln took a flatboat down the Mississippi to New Orleans. He saw slaves being badly treated and sold like animals. It made him want to try to free the slaves.

The history of the river, though, goes back much further than even Abraham Lincoln's day.

The Mississippi's widest point is 3.5 miles, just north of Clinton, Iowa.

The Making of the Mississippi

About 2 million years ago, Earth's climate became very cold. Large sheets of ice called **glaciers** spread southward from the North Pole. These glaciers carried tons of rock and soil with them as they covered large parts of North America.

Then slowly the Earth became warmer. The ice began to melt, leaving behind the rocks and soil. The water from the melting ice needed somewhere to go.

This is how the Mississippi was born. Water rushed down the river, moving rocks and soil out of its path. Some of the soil left on the banks of the river became good farmland.

Some soil built up mud banks that formed **swamps**. Many of these swamps can be found near the river's end at the Gulf of Mexico.

Wildlife on the Mississippi

In Minnesota, where the river begins, snow or frost can cover the ground for six months of the year. In Louisiana, where the river ends, it is warm most of the time. Because of this, many different kinds of animals live along the Mississippi.

Thousands of birds, including geese, pelicans, and ducks, follow the river as they fly south each winter. So do monarch butterflies, which spend the winter in Mexico.

The clear, cold waters of the river travel through many forests in the north. Beavers can be found there, building their dams of twigs and logs. There are also deer, moose, and black bears living in the forests.

In Missouri and Kentucky the river forests change with trees suited to the warmer climate.

The American alligator is often seen along the southern end of the Mississippi River.

The muddy Missouri River connects with the Mississippi near the city of St. Louis, Missouri. Fish that can live in the muddy water, like carp and catfish, are found in this part of the river. White-tailed deer and wild turkeys live near the riverbanks.

Many more unusual plants and animals make their home in the Mississippi **Delta** in Louisiana. In the Delta the American alligator is king!

The alligator, Louisiana's state reptile, can weigh 400 to 500 pounds.

Nutrias have webbed feet and long tails.

The warm climate of Louisiana makes it a perfect home for many animals. Have you ever seen a frog as big as a football or a 10-foot-long fish? You can find either one in the many swamps that are part of the Mississippi River in this area.

In **prehistoric** times **mammoths** roamed these swamps. Today animals such as bobcats, raccoons, and nutrias, which are large rodents, live in the swamps and on riverbanks.

Mammoths looked like huge elephants with trunks and tusks up to 13 feet long.

The armadillo is one of the strangest-looking animals living near the Mississippi. It is covered with bony plates, like armor, that protect it. It is active mostly at night but may also be seen on cloudy, dark days.

Armadillos live in the south central and southeastern United States. They eat mostly insects, worms, and lizards, which are plentiful near the Mississippi.

The armadillo eats insects and worms. If frightened, it digs a hole and hides underground.

Peter Lourie and Ernie LaPrairie traveled the length of the Mississippi River by canoe, from Minnesota to New Orleans, Louisiana.

It's sometimes hard to figure out what kinds of animals are swimming in the Mississippi's dark water. Peter Lourie and Ernie LaPrairie traveled down the river in a canoe. One night something made a loud splash. Peter jokingly called it a Mississippi mud monster. "I always had the feeling of something large looming just beneath the canoe," he said. "I wondered what mysteries lay in the mud." They never saw what caused that splash, though.

The Working River

Peter Lourie is right about mysterious things hidden in the river's muddy bottom, though. There are many wrecks of boats and barges down there.

In the 1800s steamboats were important for travel and trade. Steamboats carried traders and soldiers. They also carried goods such as hay, corn, and cotton, and animals such as cows and horses.

Steamboats such as this one could be found traveling up and down the Mississippi in the 1800s.

Many steamboat wrecks still lie in the mud on the bottom of the Mississippi.

Many steamboats sank. Sparks from their **boilers** sometimes started fires. Sometimes they'd hit another boat. Sunken rocks and sandbars also made river travel unsafe.

Strong river **rapids** also caused problems. In the 1920s the government decided to do something to make river travel safer. The U.S. Army began building **locks** and dams on the river.

By 1867, 133 boats had sunk in the stretch of the river that ran from St. Louis, Missouri, to Cairo, Illinois.

Locks let a boat go from one level of water to another. When going from a lower to a higher level, the boat enters the lock and the gates are closed. Then water is pumped in. The water slowly raises the boat until it reaches the higher level. Then the gates are opened, and the boat can go on its way.

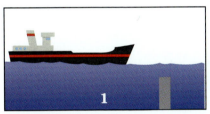

As the boat approaches the lock, the gate is lowered.

The boat enters the lock and the gates are closed.

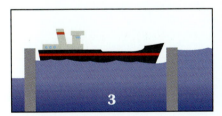

Water is pumped into the lock.

When the water is high enough, the gate is lowered and the boat moves to the next level.

Rock walls called wing dams have also been built out into the river from its banks. They make the water run fast between them, washing away mud that could make the river bottom too high. When mud builds up the river bottom, it is easy for boats to run aground. Wing dams prevent that from happening.

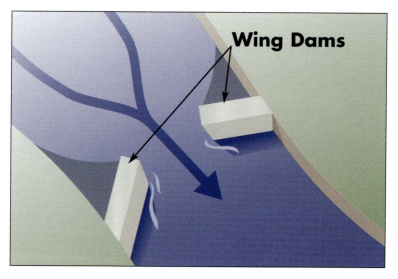

Wing dams force the water into a narrow channel.

A tugboat, or "tug," pushes 18 barges up the Mississippi.

Many large ships sail on the river, including cargo ships, tankers, steamboats, barges, and tugboats. Heavy loads of goods such as coal, steel, and foods are carried on large, flat barges pushed or pulled upriver by tugboats.

Moving goods by ship costs much less than using trains or trucks. It is not always as safe, though.

Often 20 or more barges are tied together with strong wire ropes.

Many animals rely on the Mississippi for their habitats, such as this beaver.

Some ships carry oil and chemicals. If they sink or get damaged, the contents can spill into the river and harm its wildlife.

As more and more people began to live near the river, many trees were cut down. This meant that many animals lost their habitats. Then in the 1950s people began to plant trees near the river to soak up flood waters. These forests are now providing new homes for turkeys, eagles, beavers, and deer.

Floods

Even with trees to help soak up extra water, floods can still happen. The Missouri River joins the Mississippi just north of St. Louis. The Ohio River joins at Cairo, Illinois. In the spring too much rain and melting snow in northern states can run extra water into all three rivers. In 1927 and in 1951 this caused flood problems.

The worst flooding, though, was in 1993. Winter rains and melting snow had already soaked the ground. Heavy rains and fierce thunderstorms in the summer created flooding. Then the Mississippi and other nearby rivers spilled over their banks.

Towns, cities, and farms were under water. Floods covered 17,000 square miles of land. Fifty people died and about 70,000 lost their homes. Minnesota, Iowa, Illinois, and Missouri suffered the most damage.

Sandbags piled along the riverbanks can help hold back the rising flood waters.

Fifteen-year-old Mark Stookey and his friends tried to fight the rising river. "We took turns filling bags with sand, tying them, and loading them onto pickup trucks," he said. They made a wall of the sturdy sandbags on the riverbank, but nothing could stop the river.

After the flood hit, Mark and his father rowed in a boat down Fifth Street in Des Moines, Iowa. "I'll never forget the shock of seeing all that water," said Mark.

The flood lasted many months. People who had lost much showed great courage and strength. A few even found humor in it. Nan's Nummies Cookie Shoppe in West Des Moines sold brownies they called "Flood Mud."

"I used to call them Mississippi Mud Bars," said shop owner Nancy Earll. "But that was before the flood. I think the new name is better."

Davenport, Iowa's downtown area during the 1993 flood.

Levees such as this one help hold back flood waters.

The 1993 flood probably could not have been prevented. It was very unusual for states near the Mississippi to receive that much rain. To prevent future floods, though, more **levees** have been built along the river.

A levee is a wall built along the banks of a river to keep it from flooding. In many river towns the levees are higher than the streets. Some are 15 to 30 feet high.

Even with a levee, escaping from a flood can still be a matter of luck. "We live by a levee that broke," said 11-year-old Signe Newman, also of Des Moines. "We were lucky because we have a two-story house on a hill, so we just had some water in our basement. But four houses away from us, the water was over the roof." Over the years there have been many changes in the Mississippi. People have built levees and dams to stop flooding and prevent shipwrecks. They've dug canals to connect it with other rivers. More people use the river now. This is good news for those who need to ship goods, but not for wildlife and fishermen.

More people living along the river means more **pollution** from fertilizers, chemicals, and trash. More ships using the river also cause more pollution. This problem has been growing for years. For a long time many people thought nothing could be done about it.

Cleaning the River

Chad Pregracke is working to change that. He grew up by the Mississippi, in Illinois. As a boy he swam in the river. He found things he didn't like—things such as worn tires, old shoes, and even a lawn mower!

"Garbage is not the biggest problem the river faces," Chad says, "but it's the one I can make a dent in myself. . . . When I started out, a lot of people thought I was nuts."

No one thinks Chad is nuts today. He sails up and down the river collecting garbage. In 1998 he got a whole town to help him!

"We had about 25 volunteers who went out with Chad," said Len Williams, of Burlington, Iowa, who helped in the cleanup. "It was extremely hot, we got awfully dirty, and there were a lot of bugs." For Len and Chad it was worth it. "We cleaned a couple of miles of shoreline. It really went over well," Len added.

The people of Winona, Minnesota, have formed a group called the Mississippi River Revival. In 2001, 70 people came to help clean up the river near Winona. Director Sol Simon says, "That's a good sign. People are taking care of the river."

Many people feel like Chad, who says, "I'm going to do it right, and I'm going to finish it." With people like Chad at work, "Old Man River" will keep rolling along.

Chad Pregracke is determined to help clean up the Mississippi River.

Glossary

boiler   a tank that heats water until it turns to steam that can be used to run an engine

delta   a triangle-shaped piece of land at the mouth of a large river formed by deposits of soil and sand

glacier   a large mass of ice and snow that moves very slowly down a mountain or across land until it melts

levee   a sturdy wall or bank built along a river to keep it from overflowing

locks   enclosed sections of canals or rivers with gates at each end

mammoths   a type of large elephant with shaggy, brown hair and long, curved tusks that lived long ago

pollution   wastes or poisonous substances in air, water, or land

prehistoric   of the time before history was written

rapids   parts of rivers where the water moves very quickly

swamps   wet, marshy lands